It Only Takes a Spark

40 Active Faith-Building Talks

Kim Marxhausen

CONCORDIA PUBLISHING HOUSE • SAINT LOUIS

To Dr. J.D. and Esther Weinhold from
your first experiment.
Thank you for keeping the Word an
active ingredient in my life.

5 6 7 8 9 10 11 12 13   13 12 11 10 09 08 07 06 05

Contents

Introduction

When I was a child, my dad, a science professor, gave a chapel lesson at our school using a nifty experiment that neutralized an acid and base solution. The black-and-red solution turned clear and the lesson of Jesus' blood washing our sin away went right from our brains straight to our hearts. The impact of that lesson is the reason for this book.

Each devotion in this book uses a science experiment to illustrate a faith concept. The experiments are a creative, concrete way to teach children about God's world while explaining our relationship with our heavenly Father. As you use this book, keep these things in mind:

1. These devotions have been written in sections to allow for some flexibility in presenting to different age groups. When using these devotions with younger children, omit the results section and explain the experiment at their level of understanding. Older children will want to know why the experiment worked and will be better able to handle the terminology.

2. Two Bible verses have been selected for each devotion. Use the first verse for younger audiences and both verses when working with older children.

3. Read through the directions in their entirety before choosing a devotion. Many experiments can be done on the spot, but some must be prepared ahead of time.

4. Due to various factors such as humidity levels and differences in materials, some results may vary. You may need to make minor adjustments to achieve the desired effect.

5. Try the experiment ahead of time. These experiments were chosen for their simplicity but the best results are achieved with practice.

6. While the devotions can be read to a group of children, you will be more effective if you summarize the devotion in your own words.

Use these simple science experiments to give your students interactive, visual lessons that give them insight into the ways God has blessed them.

1 Can You Prove God Exists?

You believe because of faith.

Active Ingredient

Hebrews 11:1, 1 Peter 1:8–9

Hypothesis

What would you say if a friend asked you to prove that God existed? You can't use any of your five senses to prove Him. You can't prove Him with a math formula or detect Him with a turbocharged supersonic radar God detector. You know that God is real but *how* do you know it?

It is useful to think of our world as being made up of molecules. But if molecules exist, they are so small that we cannot see them with even the most powerful microscope. Scientists have developed a model of the world made of molecules by watching what they do. Here is an experiment that makes us think that molecules are real and always moving.

Lab Equipment

- A clear glass with hot water
- A clear glass with cold water
- Food coloring

Procedure

Set glasses on a level surface and allow to sit until water is still. Add one or two drops of food coloring to each glass but do not stir the water.

Results

The food coloring drops will first sink to the bottom of the glass. Gradually, the food coloring will spread throughout the glass. Scientists think it is the movement of the water molecules that spreads the food coloring throughout the water. The science model for molecules shows that molecules move slower when they are cold and faster when they are hot. This may be why the food coloring in the hot water spreads faster.

Application

Scientists cannot prove that molecules exist because molecules cannot be seen. Even an electron microscope will only show patterns, not real molecules. Many different experiments like the one you tried today can best be explained with a model or an idea that the world is made of molecules, but scientists can't see molecules—how do they know molecules exist?.

Christians cannot prove that God exists using math or chemistry or labaratory experiments. You suspect that He exists because of the beautiful and complex world He made, but even this is not scientific.proof. Even though you can't prove scientifically that God is real, you *know* He is. That special kind of *knowing* is called faith. Faith is a gift from God. Without faith you can't believe or understand God. With faith you know that God is with you and loves you.

Let's look at another example of faith. At Christmas we hear two stories. One story is about a baby in a manger, the other about a fat man in a red suit. When you were little, you probably believed both stories. As you grew older you became suspicious about the truth behind Santa. Something told you even magic couldn't make a fat man fit through a tiny chimney.

Even though you figured out that the Santa story is just pretend, you still believe that Jesus was born in Bethlehem and laid in a manger. There are some parts of that story that are hard to imagine, like a sky full of angels and a star that leads Wise Men to Bethlehem from a different country. These things are not everyday happenings, yet you know they happened. You believe in what you have not seen because of the gift of faith worked in you by the Holy Spirit at your Baptism.

You can't prove your faith exists; yet you know it is there. Your faith is a powerful gift from God. As you grow and study God's Word, the Holy Spirit will continue to make your faith grow. God does exist. You believe it!

2 God at the Center

Repentance means turning back to God.

Active Ingredient

Joel 2:13, Acts 3:19

Hypothesis

Have you noticed that whenever there is a toy prize in a box of cereal, it always manages to find its way to the bottom of the box? In this experiment you will find yourself always returning to the center.

Lab Equipment

- A yardstick
- A volunteer

Procedure

Ask the volunteer to stand with her hands about two feet apart with palms turned inward. Center the yardstick on top of her hands. Ask the volunteer to bring her hands together to see if the stick can be made to be unbalanced. Try again. This time, do not center the yardstick on the volunteer's hands. Is it possible for your volunteer to bring her hands together at a point other than the center? Is it possible to slide hands together in such a way as to upset the balance of the stick?

Results

Friction is caused when the volunteer moves her hands along the underside of the yardstick. The heavier the weight, the more friction is caused and movement becomes more difficult. If the yardstick is not centered, the longer portion of the stick is heavier and the hand beneath it will not slide as easily. The hand on the shorter end moves easily and therefore slides to meet the other hand at the center.

Application

Just as the volunteer's hands kept coming back to the center of the yardstick, so you also need to keep coming back to your heavenly Father. Returning to God is called repentance.

The prodigal son tried to run away from his father. He took his money and spent it until he had nothing left and no one to love and care for him. He went back to his father for forgiveness. And forgiveness was freely given.

When you sin, you run away from your heavenly Father. Not only does He wait patiently for your return but He sent His only Son to make it possible for you to return. Each time you sin you can go back to the Father and receive forgiveness.

The second part of repentance is to change your behavior. The Father willingly forgives, the Son makes forgiveness possible, and the Spirit works change in your heart. Whenever sin causes you to wander, go back to the center and find forgiveness in your heavenly Father.

3 Make the Impossible Possible

Jesus makes heaven possible.

Active Ingredient

Matthew 19:26, Romans 3:23–24

Hypothesis

Clean your room! Stop hitting your brother! Finish your homework! Did you forget to walk the dog? Get your dirty socks off the living room floor! Does this song sound familiar? Can you think of a few more verses?

Life is full of many rules and regulations. There are rules at school and rules at home. There are rules at the arcade and rules on the ball field. There are rules in the mall and even rules in the clubs kids make for themselves. Your life is better if you can keep track of all these rules and follow them. But that is easier said than done.

God gave you only 10 rules. He gave you the Ten Commandments. Ten rules doesn't sound so bad, does it? The problem is you are to follow these 10 rules perfectly. You can't slip up even once. Because you were born a sinner, this is an impossible task.

Here is an experiment that makes the impossible possible. Using only the thread, and without tying a knot, it will be possible to pick up an ice cube.

Lab Equipment

- A full glass of water
- An ice cube
- A 6″ piece of thread
- Salt

Procedure

Put the ice cube in the glass of water and set the thread over the cube so its ends dangle over the edges of the glass. Wait a minute and try to pick up the ice by lifting the string. Can you think of any way to pick up the ice cube? Maybe if you could get the thread under the ice cube and cradle it. It looks like an impossible task.

Put the thread across the ice cube once again. This time sprinkle a little salt on the thread and the ice. Now wait a minute or two and try gently lifting the ice cube with the thread. You have done what you thought was impossible.

Results

Water normally freezes at 32° F (0° C). Adding salt to the water lowers the freezing point so the ice melts just enough to refreeze around the string.

Application

God expects you to follow His Ten Commandments perfectly. This is impossible for you because of your sin. Jesus made the impossible possible when He was on earth. He followed all of God's laws perfectly, and He didn't even use a trick. Because Jesus lived a perfect life and because He gave up His perfect life by dying on the cross, God will give you a perfect life in heaven. It's a free gift, no strings attached.

You can bet the thief on the cross next to Jesus broke a few rules. He messed up enough to find himself being executed for his sins. But this thief had the gift of faith.

God gives you 10 rules and an order to follow them perfectly. But just like a little salt helped you lift the ice cube, God adds the gift of grace to this experiment. He loves you no matter what. Yes, there are rules and yes, you should follow them and yes, you will break the rules. But, when you mess up, grace and the love of your Savior are waiting there to rescue you.

4 How Do You Measure Up?

The love of God makes you whole.

Active Ingredient

Romans 4:7, Ephesians 3:17–19

Hypothesis

How do you know if you "measure up" to God's standard? It is an honor to be called a child of God, but how do you know if you rate the title? Are you smart enough? Kind enough? Generous enough? Cute enough? How good is good enough?

Here is a measuring problem: You need to measure a tree that is taller than the roof of the church and all you have to do it with is a couple of yardsticks. How is it going to get done? Maybe you could climb the tree and measure it yard by yard as you slide down the trunk. If you had a kite you could fly it to the top and mark your string. Then bring the kite down to the ground and measure how much string you let out. What if you held the yardstick in front of you and looked at the tree with one eye, then slowly walk backward until the tree looks like it is only one yard high? There has got to be a better way.

Lab Equipment

- A tree
- A sunny day
- Two yardsticks

Procedure

Hold one yardstick on end and make sure your shadow does not cover the shadow of the yardstick. Measure the shadow of the yardstick. If the shadow of the yardstick is one yard long, then measuring the shadow of the tree will tell you the height of the tree. If the shadow of the yardstick is not equal to the length of the yardstick, you will need to do a little math. Measure the shadow of each in inches, then multiply the length of the tree's shadow by 36. Then divide by the length of the shadow of the yardstick. Your result is the tree's height in inches.

Results

At the right time of the day, the tree and its shadow form the equal legs of an isosceles triangle. If the yardstick "measures up" to its shadow, then the tree will also. This method is most accurate when measuring a tree with a pointed top. The shadow of a round tree may be the shadow of the side of the tree, not the top.

Application

A yardstick works to measure a tree, but children of God are measured in a different way. We are measured with a yardstick called the Law. If you want to know how well you "measure up," you have to measure yourself with the Ten Commandments. How well do you do the things God asks you to do?

God asks us to follow the Ten Commandments, to love Him more than we love anyone or anything, and to love our neighbor as ourselves. You can and should try to do these things, but the measure of your good deeds is not equal to the measure of the Law. You don't make an isosceles triangle. You fall short every time.

The Bible verse talks about how wide and long and high and deep is the love of Christ. Christ's love for you "measures up" to the demands of the Law. He fulfilled the law perfectly. God still commands you to fulfill the law too. And while you try to do that, He is at work in you to help you *want* to obey Him and love those around you. You are "filled to the measure of all the fullness of God" because of what Christ has done for you. With Christ standing behind you and casting His shadow over your life, you "measure up."

5 Don't Hide in the Shadows

Stay away from the shadow of temptation.

Active Ingredient

Hebrews 2:18, Matthew 5:16

Hypothesis

It is aggravating when someone stands in your light while you are reading or blocks your view of the TV screen while you are watching your favorite show. This experiment shows why light cannot go around obstacles in its path.

Lab Equipment

- A table
- Dominoes
- A flashlight

Procedure

Stand the dominoes on the table. Using the flashlight, try different light angles to observe shadows. Which shadows are the longest? Which are the shortest? Is it possible to shine the light to make no shadow at all?

Result

Light travels in straight lines called rays. Light rays are stopped by objects in their path because they cannot bend around them. A shadow is a dark spot left because the light rays were unable to get there. Moving the light source can make a shadow larger or smaller.

Application

Temptations can be like large objects in your path. It can be hard to get around them. They are always there for you to look at or think about. Sometimes temptations are hard to resist. They can be like an object that casts a shadow on your heart.

Think about the temptations in your life. Are you tempted to tease classmates? Pester your brother or sister? Forget to do your chores? Steal small things from the store? Or maybe cheat on a spelling test? Every day the devil puts temptations to sin in your path. But you have a strong weapon against temptation—the Holy Spirit. He came into your heart when you were baptized and He works to turn you away from the temptation of sin.

The Bible says the best way to fight temptation is to get away from it. If you are close to temptation, it is hard for your light to shine around it. Prayer is always a good way to fight temptation. Prayer reminds you that you have God to help you resist sin. You are not expected to, and you can't fight sin on your own.

Remember that when Jesus was here on earth He fought temptation. He knows what a struggle it can be to do the right thing, and that is why He sent His Spirit to keep you safe from sin. So, let your light shine before men.

The Sin Neutralizer

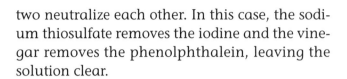

The blood of Jesus washes away sin.

Active Ingredient

John 3:16, Jeremiah 31:34

Hypothesis

Movies that take place in outer space often use a weapon of some sort that completely vaporizes the enemy. After a reign of terror, a vicious alien is neutralized by a small weapon in the hands of the story's hero. This experiment will require some unusual materials and the help of someone who knows how to use them, but the effect is memorable. The original illustration was created by Dr. Wilfred Kruse.

Lab Equipment

- **Solution A** (Use 20 ml of the final solution)
  100 ml vinegar
  1 tsp. starch
  10 drops (1 ml) iodine
- **Solution B** (Use 15 ml of final solution)
  50 ml sodium hydroxide
  10 drops (1 ml) phenolphthalein
  10 drops (1 ml) sodium thiosulfate

Procedure

These items and the expertise needed to prepare them can be obtained in a high school chemistry lab. It will take some practice and the amounts of each ingredient may be a little different, depending on the strengths of the ingredients you use. Solution A is a dark blue acid solution. Solution B is a base and is red. When the two solutions are mixed, the combination of the two will turn clear.

Results

Acids and bases are chemical opposites. When solution A is mixed with solution B, the two neutralize each other. In this case, the sodium thiosulfate removes the iodine and the vinegar removes the phenolphthalein, leaving the solution clear.

Application

The dark solution represents your sin. The iodine turns black in reaction to the starch, and your words and actions are black in reaction to the sinful nature of your heart.

The red solution represents the saving blood of Jesus Christ. The shedding of Jesus' blood is the only thing that will rid your heart of the stain of sin. The red solution of Jesus' blood forgives you of your sins just as the mixture of these solutions turns clear.

When you forgive a friend who has hurt you, it is hard to forget what he has done. Sometimes hurt feelings last a long time. When God forgives you, the sin is gone. He does not remember it and save it and use it against you later. The sin has been neutralized. The blood of Jesus makes your heart clear and perfect before God.

7 Turn Your Heart to Glass

Baptism changes you.

Active Ingredient

Acts 2:38, 2 Corinthians 3:18

Hypothesis

Heat can change a solid into a liquid or a liquid into a gas. Changes in our lives require a different process. What happens when a baby is baptized? We say he or she has become a child of God. But what does that mean? When people are baptized they don't look any different. Their bodies don't change. They are still the same people, yet something is different.

In this experiment you will change the crystals of sugar into a liquid and back to a different kind of solid. It will still be sugar, but it will be different.

Lab Equipment

- A greased cookie sheet
- 1 cup of sugar
- A stainless steel cooking pot
- A large wooden spoon

Procedure

Put the greased cookie sheet into the refrigerator to cool. Pour the sugar into the cooking pot and turn the burner on low. Stir the sugar slowly and constantly while it is heating. After about 10 minutes you will notice that the sugar has begun to stick together in lumps. Keep stirring until the tan lumps melt into a brown liquid. When all the sugar is melted, remove the liquid from the heat and pour it onto the greased cookie sheet.

Results

Heat was the only thing needed to change the sugar crystals into liquid. When it cooled and returned to a solid, it became evident that a permanent change happened. The crystals have now formed a smooth solid.

Factories make glass out of sand in a similar process. The sand is heated at very high temperatures until it melts into a liquid. The liquid is cooled until it hardens into the glass we use in our windows. Heat is what changes the sand into something we can see through.

Application

At Baptism God makes a change happen in your heart. He doesn't use heat or chemicals to change you, God uses forgiveness and the Holy Spirit to make a wonderful change in your life.

The sugar is still sugar after you heat it. It still tastes like sugar, but it is in a different form. When a child of God is baptized, he or she still looks the same and even acts the same but something is different. God uses water and His Word to show you that He forgives your sins when you are baptized. The forgiveness of sins promises you the gift of eternal life.

The changes that God works in your heart through Baptism make other changes in your life as well. The Holy Spirit builds a faith in God and strengthens that faith with the Word of God. The Holy Spirit helps you to learn about God and gives you the courage and joy to tell others about what Jesus has done for you. If what you really need is a window, sand is not a useful product. As sand you may not be very useful, but as glass you will reflect the glory of the Lord.

Turn Sugar to Crystal

Use patience, perseverance, and prayer.

Active Ingredient

Psalm 40:1, Luke 11:9–10

Hypothesis

Waiting is one of the toughest things a kid is expected to do. You wait in line, wait your turn, wait around, wait for a little brother, wait a minute, lie in wait to ambush a friend with a water balloon, wait until you're bigger, and wait until your father comes home. When you are waiting for something important, the wait can seem like forever.

Here is a project that requires a little waiting. With some patience you will finally see the results.

Lab Equipment

- 1 cup of water
- A clear jar or glass
- 2–4 cups of sugar
- A pencil
- A piece of cotton string

Procedure

Boil the water and remove from heat. Add 2 cups of sugar and stir. If all the sugar dissolves, add more until sugar settles in the bottom of the pan. When the water has cooled a little bit, pour the solution into the glass jar. Tie the string around the pencil. Rub some sugar crystals onto the string so they stick to it. Set the pencil over the top of the jar so the string drops into the water and sugar solution. Set the jar somewhere where it will be undisturbed until crystals form (two or three days).

Results

When you add sugar to water, the small sugar crystals break down and saturate the water, making it a sugar solution. Warm water holds more sugar than cool water. When it cools, it becomes supersaturated, which means the water can no longer hold that much sugar. The sugar comes out of the solution and forms new crystals joining the smaller crystals on the string.

Application

There is a time in your faith life when you have to wait. God always answers your prayers, but sometimes He doesn't give you the answer right away. Sometimes God's answer is "wait."

When Jesus taught the disciples to pray, He taught them the Lord's Prayer. He didn't stop there. He used the story of a man who had an unexpected visitor and needed some bread. Jesus said you should pray like the man who kept asking for bread until his friend finally relented and gave him what he had. In this story, Jesus teaches you to have patience and persistence when you pray. He also shows you that God is your Father and that He welcomes your persistence. He does not get angry when you ask Him again and again. He loves you.

If the answer to your prayer is "wait," be patient and keep praying. With patience your sugar solution turned into rock candy. With patience you will see God turn your prayer into something good.

Foaming at the Heart

God knows your potential.

Active Ingredient

2 Chronicles 1:12, Psalm 81:10

Hypothesis

Some days nothing goes right. The score at the top of your spelling test, the yogurt spilled inside your lunch bag, the sad face on the computer screen in the computer lab, and the looks of disappointment on the faces of your teammates as the soccer ball whizzes past you aren't helping you to feel good about yourself today. Some days make you wonder, if you can't handle grade school is there hope for you as an adult?

It is hard to tell a person's potential by looking at him. It is also hard to tell what a liquid can do if we only *look* at it. Let's test a couple of liquids another way.

Lab Equipment

- 4 clear glasses
- Water
- White vinegar
- 2 teaspoons of baking soda

Procedure

Fill two glasses half full of water. Add two teaspoons of baking soda to one glass of water. Stir well so the baking soda dissolves completely and the solution looks like water again. Fill the third and fourth glasses half full of white vinegar.

Pour one glass of vinegar into the glass with plain water and observe. Pour the second glass of vinegar into the baking soda and water solution and observe.

Results

Even though all four glasses looked as if they contained water, the results of mixing were not the same. Mixing vinegar and water did nothing but fill the glass. Adding vinegar to the baking soda solution made foam. The baking soda is a carbonate and the vinegar an acid. The combination of the two formed carbon dioxide. This gas caused the liquid to foam up and out of the glass.

Application

Looks can be deceiving. Two of the liquids mixed together were a flop. The other two had big potential. You may not feel like you have much potential to do God's work in this world, but God can see into your heart and He knows the potential He has put there. The mistakes you make, the activities that make you stumble, and the looks of disappointment pointed in your direction do not predict what gifts God has given you. It is easy to judge yourself by the standards of the world. Everyone wants to be smart, creative, good-looking, and athletic. God has a different view. He knows what is really important.

Many people in the Bible had mediocre beginnings. The brothers of David and Joseph would not have elected either of them to the top job in the land. Look at Jesus' disciples—Simon Peter, Andrew, and John were all fishermen. Fishermen were hard workers but not exactly the type predicted to be leaders. What about Matthew? Matthew was a tax collector. He was not on anyone's list of favorite people. Who would have predicted that a cheater would have the potential to write one of the gospels? Jesus did.

Some days you feel worthless. Remember that you are a child of God, and He has blessed you with special gifts. God can look into your heart and know that He has given you the potential to be a teacher or a pastor or a missionary. He knows what work is planned for you. He will be with you to help you reach that potential. Let Him add the vinegar of grace, then stand back and watch what happens.

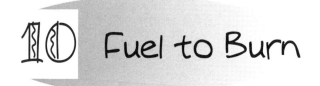

10 Fuel to Burn

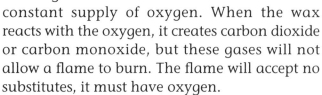

Keep your faith light burning.

Active Ingredient

Matthew 4:4, 1 Peter 2:2

Hypothesis

The song "This Little Gospel Light of Mine" talks about letting your faith shine. Your faith shines "all around the neighborhood" when you tell others about the love of Jesus.

You know your faith is a gift from God, but what keeps that candle burning? Try the following experiment to see what keeps real candles burning.

Lab Equipment

- Small votive candle
- Matches
- Saucer
- Glass jar
- Water

Procedure

Light the candle and set it on the saucer. Pour about ¼ cup of water onto the saucer. Place the glass jar, upside down, over the candle.

Results

The candle needs oxygen to burn. As the candle burns, the flame heats the air and the air expands. Some of the expanding air escapes from the jar. The candle flame is extinguished when the oxygen is consumed. When the remaining air cools, it contracts and water seeps in to replace the air that escaped earlier.

Application

For the flame to keep burning it must have a constant supply of oxygen. When the wax reacts with the oxygen, it creates carbon dioxide or carbon monoxide, but these gases will not allow a flame to burn. The flame will accept no substitutes, it must have oxygen.

The flame of faith in your heart needs fuel to burn too. Your faith grows when you hear the Word of God. The Bible is oxygen to your faith. Without God's Word, your flame is in danger of going out. With God's Word, your flame will burn brighter than ever.

In the parable of the sower, Jesus shows how God's Word grows and produces in His people who hear it and understand it. The world wants to be weeds or birds and choke out or snatch away the power of God's Word. But to a child of God, His Word is fuel that burns bright and clear.

You do not have to keep your faith under a glass to keep the world from dousing the flame. Protecting a candle under glass only serves to suffocate the flame. Keep your faith out and burning and God will protect you.

Don't forget to fuel your faith. Remember as a candle needs a constant supply of oxygen so also you need a constant supply of God's Word. When and how often do you refuel each week? Of course, there are church and Sunday school, midweek classes, chapel, vacation Bible school, and other opportunities at church. Do you refuel at home too? Family devotions and personal Bible reading will refuel your faith and keep it burning bright.

The Bible says we should be newborn babies and "crave pure spiritual milk." The flame of the candle requires the fuel of oxygen. Your faith craves the fuel of God's Word.

11 Do You Rub Off on Your Friends?

You influence people through the Holy Spirit.

Active Ingredient

Colossians 4:5–6, 1 Peter 3:15

Hypothesis

Do you influence your friends or do they influence you? If someone in your group of friends had the idea to do something wrong, would you be able to convince the group to do what was pleasing to God? If kids who don't know about God hang around with you, will they learn about God?

Find a penny and an iron nail and rub them together. Not much happened. With vinegar and a little salt you can make the copper of the penny rub off onto the iron nail.

Lab Equipment

- A glass jar
- ¼ cup vinegar
- Salt
- 10–20 pennies (well tarnished)
- Iron nail
- Scouring powder

Procedure

Pour vinegar into the jar and add a pinch of salt. Add the copper pennies, and let them stand in the jar for a few minutes. Clean the iron nail with the scouring powder. Rinse very carefully, then let the clean nail soak in the vinegar with the pennies for about 15 minutes.

Results

You will notice the nail is now covered with copper and the pennies are very clean. The vinegar is an acid that cleaned the copper pennies. The copper lost from the tarnish of the pennies formed a new compound with the vinegar called copper acetate. This compound coated the iron nail with copper.

Application

As a child of God, you are a penny and your friends who do not know Jesus are iron nails. However, simply hanging around them does not cause your faith to rub off on your friends. The copper tarnish will not rub off onto the nails without the chemical reaction of the vinegar acid. Your faith will not rub off on people who don't believe without help from God.

God is the vinegar that makes the chemical change happen. God made you, chose you as His child, and gave you faith. When you live among people who have not heard of God's wonderful gift of salvation, the Holy Spirit makes a change happen. Your life rubs off on the people around you. It is not your actions alone that witness to your friends, but rather as you live the Word and speak the Word to those around you, they will see your light shining and give praise to the Father in heaven. (See Matthew 5:16.)

It is a good idea to do your best to live a godly life. God has given us His rules for living to protect us and to show us His will. It is true that we are not very good examples to others if we give in to the temptations the world puts in front of us. But just like the penny could not give copper to the nail without the vinegar and salt, we can't rub off on people just by trying to live a good life. We can't even live a good life without God's help.

We are God's children. God uses us as tools to further His ministry on earth. God's action in us will act as vinegar and salt to clean us and cause us to share our faith with the people in our life. Remember God's Word and let your conversation and your actions be always full of grace and seasoned with salt. Go ahead—rub off on someone!

12 The Good, the Bad, and the Saved

You are in the world but not of the world.

Active Ingredient

John 3:36, Matthew 3:11–12

Hypothesis

Precious metals like gold and silver are found in the ground or in streams mixed with rocks and sand. While the rocks are worthless, the gold or silver is valuable and needs to be separated. This experiment demonstrates how something valuable can be separated from something worthless. It is the same process used to separate precious metals and minerals.

Lab Equipment

- Glass jar
- 2 tablespoons metallic glitter
- 2 tablespoons sand
- 1 cup water
- 2 tablespoons vegetable oil

Procedure

Put the glitter, sand, and water into the jar. Shake the jar to mix up the sand and glitter. Add the oil and shake vigorously. Leave jar undisturbed, allowing contents to settle. You can filter the glitter out of the oil by pouring just the oil and glitter through a coffee filter.

Results

The glitter floats to the surface of the water by clinging to the oily bubbles. The sand settles to the bottom of the jar. This is a commercial separation process called *froth flotation.* The shaking of the jar blows air into the water, creating a froth of oily bubbles. The oil does not dissolve in water and it is less dense so it floats to the surface. As it floats, it takes the glitter with it, leaving the sand to sink to the bottom.

Application

As God's children here on earth, we live in the world; yet we are separate from the ways of the world. We eat and sleep, play and learn the same as everyone around us. God separated us from the world when we were baptized. Our faith makes us different.

The glitter and the sand were mixed together in the water. By the end of the experiment, the glitter floated at the top while the sand sank to the bottom. The glitter didn't get there on its own, though. The glitter could not have floated to the top without the oil.

We can't separate ourselves from the world by trying to look or act different. Just like the glitter didn't separate from the sand because it was shiny, we can't separate from the world because we wear Christian symbols or do good things. We can wear crosses around our necks and give lots of money to the church and still be a part of the world.

Jesus is the oil that separates us from the sand. Jesus came down to our world, but He was separate from the world. We cling to Him, and He takes us to heaven. The sand will stay behind, but what is valuable to God will be separated. Jesus makes us valuable to God.

13 The Faith Test

You are known by your fruits.

Active Ingredient

1 John 4:16, Luke 6:43–45

Hypothesis

What if scientists could build equipment that would indicate if a person were bad or good? Suppose you had some kind of tricorder—like in *Star Trek*—that you could point at a person and it would tell you if she were lying or telling the truth, or whether her motives had your best interests at heart. An instrument like that could make your life simpler—or considerably more difficult. This test lets you know if some foods are healthy for you or if they are high in fat.

Lab Equipment

- Paper grocery sack
- Pencil
- Margarine
- Cookies
- Egg
- Potato chips
- Lemon
- Honey
- Oil popped popcorn
- Air popped popcorn

Procedure

Tear open the grocery sack so it lies flat. Draw a circle and label it for each food you wish to test. (Some possibilities are listed above.) Rub a small amount of each food into the correct circle. Let sit for 10 minutes, then examine each side of the paper.

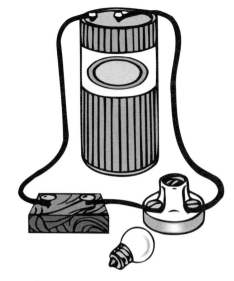

Results

When first rubbed onto the paper, each food left a wet spot. Spots made by water will dry through evaporation. Spots left by fat will not dry because they leave fat globules behind.

Application

You can't look into anyone's heart but your own. You don't even know your own heart very well. God can see into the heart of each person, and only He knows what that person is thinking.

If you are going to live in this world, you have to look out for the bad trees. You don't have a tricorder that gives you a reading on each person, but Jesus tells you to know a person by his fruits. If a person consistently does things and makes choices that are contrary to God's Word, then that is a sign of someone who is not following God's will.

People aren't all good or all bad. All people are sinners and are equally bad. However, when you are a child of God, you are also good. A child of God can and does do bad things, but he asks God to forgive him, and this forgiveness makes him good again.

Even a person who makes bad choices can be made a good tree by the forgiving love of God. As a child of God you should not let a bad tree influence you but remember that a bad tree can become good through the Good News of salvation.

Levitating Raisins

The grace of God lifts you up.

Active Ingredient

Ephesians 2:8, Romans 5:1

Hypothesis

Have you ever heard the phrase, "that sinking feeling"? It is a feeling you experience when you have made a mistake and you know there will be consequences. The raisins in this experiment have a sinking feeling but they get a little help from some bubbles.

Lab Equipment

- A clear glass
- Raisins
- Water
- 1 tablespoon baking soda
- 2 tablespoons vinegar

Procedure

Fill the glass ¾ full with water. Drop five or six raisins in the glass. Add the baking soda and stir until it dissolves. Stir in the vinegar and watch the raisins. If after a minute the raisins have not started to rise, add more vinegar.

Note: This will also work with a carbonated beverage. Use a clear soda so the raisins can be seen. No vinegar or baking soda will be necessary.

Results

The raisins sink to the bottom of the glass because they are heavier than water. The baking soda and vinegar combine to make a gas called carbon dioxide. The gas bubbles attach themselves to the raisins and float to the top, bringing the raisins along for the ride. When the gas bubbles reach the surface of the water, they pop and go into the air. The raisins no longer have their carbon dioxide life jackets and sink once again.

Application

Your sins weigh heavy on your heart. When you do something wrong, say something mean, or don't do something you knew you should have done, your heart won't let you forget it. Your conscience is God's Law written on your heart. When you do not measure up to God's Law, you feel bad.

The raisins sink to the bottom of the glass. They are too heavy to float to the top of the water alone. The gas bubbles surround the raisins and lift them up.

God forgives your sins because of what Jesus did for you. God's grace lifts you up to Him even though your guilt drags you down. God not only forgives you, but His grace lifts you up to serve Him.

When we feel bad about ourselves, we don't feel as if we can do anything good. God doesn't leave us feeling bad. He wipes away our sin and wipes away our guilt. The apostle Paul did many bad things before God chose him to serve. Paul hunted Christians, jailed them, and even watched them die, and when he learned the truth about Jesus, Paul felt very guilty.

The same grace that forgave Paul and made him God's servant is given to you. Don't just feel bad about what you've done, but know that God is faithful and just and forgives all who ask Him to. He cleans us up. Every day you ask God to forgive your sins and He does. Every day He lifts you up and enables you to be His servant.

An Erupting Faith Volcano

You can't keep the Good News a secret.

Active Ingredient

Acts 11:16, Romans 5:5

Hypothesis

Everyone knows that you can't trust a 3-year-old with the secret of what Mom is getting for Mother's Day. When you have good news from school, it's probably the first thing you announce at the dinner table. And the birthday present of a new bike just begs to be immediately shown to everyone in the neighborhood. Good news—really good news—just doesn't stay secret for long. It seems to explode right out of your heart.

This experiment makes an explosion. The liquid and the powder combine to form a gas that is hard to contain.

Lab Equipment

- ½ cup of baking soda
- ½ cup of vinegar
- A funnel
- An empty 1-quart or 1-liter bottle
- A dishpan

Procedure

Put the funnel in the 1-quart bottle and put the bottle in the dishpan. Measure the baking soda into the empty bottle. Add the vinegar all at once. The two ingredients will produce a reaction that will bubble out of the bottle.

Results

The vinegar is an acid that reacts with the carbonate in the baking soda. Together they make carbon dioxide, which is a gas. The gas expands and needs a space bigger than the bottle so it erupts out of the top and down the sides. You can see evidence of the gas in the bubbles of the foam that pours out of the bottle.

Application

You are a child of God with the gift of faith in your heart. Even if that faith is as small as a tiny seed, it can do great things. When vinegar is added to a small amount of baking soda, it grows to be too large to fit in the bottle. Your faith grows too big to stay in your heart too.

The disciples at Pentecost had faith that exploded from their hearts. They waited, praying in a room, until the Holy Spirit blessed them with faith that made them run right out into the street to tell people about the love of Jesus. Once their faith grew there was no keeping them in that little room. They had to go out and tell everyone the Good News about Jesus' death and resurrection.

Your faith is with you always, making it possible for you to believe in God. Your faith helps you to grow in your understanding of God and to follow His will for your life. When you add the Bible to your faith, just like adding vinegar to baking soda, your faith grows and grows. Reading the Bible, hearing God's Word at family devotions, in Sunday school, during worship services at church, and in school or midweek classes helps your faith grow.

The Good News that Jesus takes away our sins is news that is too good to keep locked up in our hearts. It is news that like a new bike is begging to be shared with friends immediately. Just like the disciples at Pentecost, Jesus sends us the gift of the Holy Spirit. He came into our hearts when we became children of God through our Baptism. The Holy Spirit makes our faith too big to keep in our hearts, and He helps us spread the news of Jesus to everyone.

16 Keep Them in Their Seats

You can move mountains with faith.

Active Ingredient

Matthew 17:20–21, Isaiah 7:9

Hypothesis

How much strength do you possess in your thumb? Your thumb is stronger than you think. Using only this digit, you can keep a person from standing.

Lab Equipment

- A chair
- A volunteer
- A thumb

Procedure

Ask the volunteer to sit in the chair with both feet on the floor. Make sure the volunteer keeps his back straight. (It is essential that the volunteer be sitting erect.) Place your thumb on the volunteer's forehead. Ask the volunteer to stand.

Results

Your center of gravity is in your stomach. Your head has to be past your center of gravity for you to be able to lift or stand. One person can keep another sitting by simply holding his head over his center of gravity.

Application

Jesus said you can move a mountain with your faith. As a child of God you will have many challenges in your life. God is preparing you to do His work. He wants you to learn as much as you can about Him. It is good to feed your faith through Bible reading and worship. When you have tough times to get through, remember that your faith is a gift from God and even a little faith is a powerful thing.

Faith is powerful because it depends on God, not on the person who has it. On several occasions Jesus told people that their faith had made them well. Some of these people were Gentiles who did not know much about Jesus, but their faith was strong enough to heal sicknesses or make them walk.

The disciples are another good example. Jesus was often discouraged about the weakness of the disciples' faith, yet in the book of Acts we read of amazing feats of faith performed by these same men. Because the power behind faith is God's power, nothing is impossible.

God is preparing you for big things in your life, but He has work for you to do now. You are a witness to the saving love of God in all you do and say. You witness to your friends, your neighbors, and your family. The same faith that makes it possible for you to believe in Him gives you the courage to tell others about Him.

The devil would love to knock you over, but try as he might, he cannot weaken your faith. Even faith small enough to fit in your little thumb can keep the devil down.

17 The Greatest Treasure of All

The kingdom of heaven is a treasure.

Active Ingredient

Matthew 6:20, Matthew 13:45–46

Hypothesis

There are some things you own that you wouldn't trade for anything. It could be a baseball card of your favorite player or a stuffed animal that has snuggled you through thunderstorms and bad dreams. It doesn't matter what it is but this item is a treasure to you. This experiment reveals a treasure of a different sort.

Lab Equipment

- ¼ cup hot water
- A saucer
- 2 tablespoons pickling salt

Procedure

Heat water in the microwave. Add pickling salt and stir until dissolved. Pour into saucer and set aside where it will not be disturbed. The water will evaporate and leave behind salt crystals. Different crystal shapes will form if sodium thiosulfate (photographer's hypo), alum, borax, or potassium sodium tartrate are substituted for pickling salt.

Results

You can find crystals in many nonliving substances. They are in sugar, salt, sand, ice, and diamonds. The pickling salt used in the experiment was a crystal before it was dissolved in the warm water. When the water evaporated, the larger crystal "grew" when smaller crystals attached themselves to each other in a pattern unique to that crystal.

Application

Jesus told several parables comparing the kingdom of heaven to treasure. Of all the treasures we have here on earth, our greatest treasure is the promise of the kingdom of heaven. It is worth more than all the treasures of the world combined. In fact, it is worth your life.

Jesus asked the disciples to give up everything they had to follow Him and serve Him. Jesus asks the same of you. You are to put God first and be willing to give up everything to serve Him.

You could not tell that the supersaturated solution contained a treasure. Only after the water evaporated could you see the crystals form. A Christian's treasure is not always easy for others to see. The world saves money, gems, jewelry, and other expensive items to store up as treasure. As a Christian you store up your treasure in heaven where it is safe from the world. Your treasure is the love of God and your service to Him. Your treasure is the gift of eternal life waiting for you in heaven. You did not buy your treasure; it was purchased for you with the blood of Jesus. Hold on to that treasure.

18 Tongue Mapping

You are the salt of the earth.

Active Ingredient

Mark 9:50, Hebrews 2:9

Hypothesis

Salt is a preservative and a flavor enhancer. It keeps foods from spoiling and makes the taste of food stronger. Your tongue is a taste expert. You have a team of taste buds that each have their own job to do. Try these foods and map out your tongue.

Lab Equipment

- Diagram of a tongue
- Volunteer tongues for tasting food
- Sweet, sour, and salty foods

Procedure

On poster board draw a map of the human tongue without the taste labels. Ask a volunteer to taste one item at a time to determine which parts of the tongue detect sweet, sour, and salty tastes. Check with the tongue map in this book. God made each of us unique so tongues may vary.

Results

For most people, salty and sour tastes are detected on the sides of the tongue and sweet on the tip. We also taste salty on the tip, and some people taste it in the middle of the tongue. The area in the back of the tongue will detect bitter tastes. That is why you don't taste bitter medicine until it is almost all the way down. Sweet taste buds are on the tip of the tongue. which makes lollipops and ice-cream cones more enjoyable. And if you have ever sucked a lemon wedge or a dill pickle, you have tickled the sour taste buds on the side of your tongue. It is interesting to note that acidic foods often taste sour and basic foods can be described as bitter tasting.

Because our taste buds are somewhat separated, we are able to discern different tastes. If the taste buds were mixed up, foods would likely taste very much alike. Our taste buds allow us to enjoy foods and to pick which ones we like and don't like.

Application

Salt was a valuable commodity in Jesus' time. There were no refrigerators or freezers to store meat; so salt was used to keep meat from spoiling. Salt was even used as a form of payment instead of money. When Jesus called His followers *salt,* it was a compliment.

Jesus told His followers to be *salt* and be at peace with each other. Even God's children argue with each other. If we are salt and are at peace, we are working to preserve our relationship with each other. Sin will destroy a relationship, but love will preserve it. Jesus wants us to show Christian love for each other.

Salt is also a flavor enhancer. More of your tongue is devoted to tasting salt than any other taste. Christian love is a life enhancer. Working, playing, and worshiping with people you love makes that work, play, and worship all the more enjoyable. The love God gives us for each other makes our lives better.

The taste buds in the back of your tongue are reserved for the taste of bitterness. This is not an enjoyable taste. In fact we use the term bitter to describe feelings and events we do not enjoy. Jesus tasted the most bitter taste of all. He tasted death so we might live. Because Jesus had this most wonderful love for us and because this love fills our hearts, we are able to love the people around us with a Christian love. It is only because of Jesus that we can be *salt.*

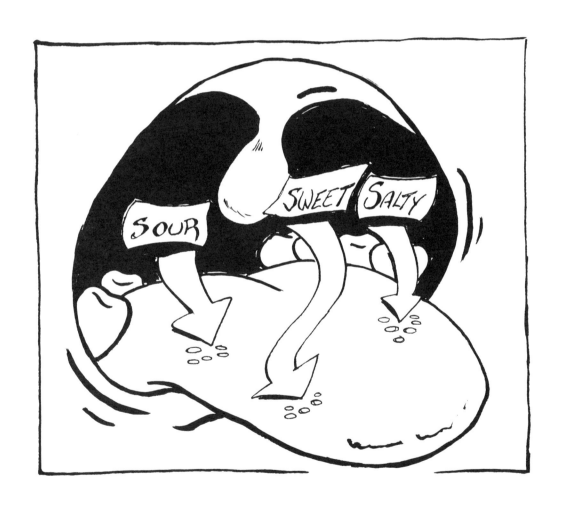

Stand strong against the world.

Active Ingredient

1 Corinthians 16:13, Romans 11:20

Hypothesis

How strong are you? Hold out your hand with your palm up. Believe it or not, you are holding nearly 100 pounds of air. Give this experiment a try to see how strong air is.

Lab Equipment

- A table
- A wooden ruler
- Newspaper

Procedure

Place the ruler on the table, with several inches hanging over the edge of the table. Fold a large sheet of newspaper to make a double sheet and spread it over the ruler so the paper lies flat along the table edge. Hit the part of the ruler that sticks out over the edge of the table as hard as you can.

Results

This experiment catches you by surprise. You would expect that when the ruler is hit the newspaper would go flying or rip in half. Instead the paper holds the ruler in place.

The paper is not working alone. On top of the newspaper is about two tons of air. The air above the paper pushes down with almost 15 pounds per square inch of weight on every square inch of newspaper surface. God has made our bodies strong enough that we do not feel the weight of air. But air does have weight.

Application

The influence of the world in our lives has weight too. You may not always notice it, but the world creeps into everything you see, hear, and read. Think about the TV, movies, or video games you have watched or played in the last week. Did you see violence, hear bad words, play a game that involved killing or hurting someone? You can get used to the world around you and neglect to feel its weight on your life.

The Bible verse tells us to be on our guard and stand strong. We are to be aware of the influence of the world and be strong in standing against it. Watch for the bad influences of the world—cigarettes, drugs, alcohol, inappropriate relationships, etc.—be courageous and stand firm in your faith. This is not easy when the people you are standing firm against are your friends.

Of course, you do not stand firm alone. God covers you and protects you as you go out into the world. Jesus is with you and shows you how to fight the influence of the world. The Holy Spirit, who has been with you from your Baptism, blesses your faith and keeps you strong. How strong are you? As a Christian with His blessing you are as strong as you need to be.

20 The Mysterious Breaking String

The grace of God makes you strong.

Active Ingredient

Philippians 4:13, 2 Corinthians 12:9

Hypothesis

There is nothing like watching a professional athlete to make you feel weak. All you have to do is compare the size of your muscles to those of a weight lifter or a football player and suddenly you feel small and insignificant. In this experiment the weak can be strong.

Lab Equipment

- Medium-sized hardcover book
- Thread
- String

Procedure

Tie the string around the middle of the book. Use a knot so it holds firmly. Cut two lengths of thread long enough to go around the book. Tie one length of thread to the string on the top of the book. Tie another to the string on the bottom. Suspend the book in the air by holding the top thread. You may want to protect your hand with a glove. If you pull on the bottom thread, which thread will break: the one bearing the weight of the book or the one being pulled? Give a short sharp pull on the bottom thread.

Results

You might expect the top thread to break because it is supporting the weight of the book. In fact, if you pull in a slow and steady fashion, the top thread will break. A short sharp pull will result in the bottom thread breaking instead.

The key to the breaking thread has to do with inertia. Inertia is the tendency for an object to stay put unless a force causes it to move. It's kind of like your big brother watching TV; nothing will move him until Mom makes him get up and take out the garbage.

If you pull the thread quickly, you will not upset the inertia of the book and since the book has not moved, no extra force is applied to the top thread and the bottom thread breaks. The inertia of the book kept the top thread from breaking.

Application

If you stare up at the stars at night, you can feel small and insignificant. When you see the beauty of the world God made, you can feel unimportant. God made the world in six days. He can do anything. What can you do?

Without God's help the answer to that question is "nothing." With God's help the answer is "anything." God uses us to spread His Word even though we are weak. He makes us strong. In fact, it is better to realize that we are weak so we remember that without God we can do nothing. Whatever we accomplish in life is because of the grace of God and His blessings to us.

21 Balloon in a Bottle

God protects you.

Active Ingredient

Isaiah 43:1, Psalm 91:9–10

Hypothesis

Has a thunderstorm ever made you pull the covers over your head? Did you ever crawl up on Dad's lap when a movie scene turned scary? Maybe you were the one holding the kindergarten teacher's hand for the first three days of school. Certain things in this world make us feel protected.

In this experiment it may look as if the balloon is being protected by the glass, but looks can be deceiving.

Lab Equipment

- Balloon
- Glass soda bottle or a plastic 20-ounce clear bottle
- A volunteer

Procedure

Insert the balloon into the bottle and stretch the balloon opening back over the bottle mouth. Ask a volunteer to blow up the balloon while it is in the bottle.

Results

You are not able to blow up the balloon while it is inside the bottle. The air inside the bottle is trapped because the balloon seals the opening. To allow the balloon to expand, the air inside the bottle would need to escape. At that point the balloon could expand to take up the space left by the departed air.

Application

The glass bottle is strong. Because it surrounds the balloon, it appears as if it protects it. However, it is the air trapped in the bottle that prevents the balloon from being inflated.

You look to the people and things in your life for protection. Bicycle helmets, knee pads, shin guards—all these things help to prevent injury. When you were small, your parents seemed strong enough to save you from anything. Dad's strong arms reassured you that it was okay to be in the deep end of the pool. A kiss from Mom instantly healed any ouchie.

God has blessed us with people and things that protect us from the dangers of the world. But just as the glass bottle could do little to protect the balloon without the air pressure, air bags and shoulder pads are not useful without God.

God loves you and protects you like a father. He doesn't want you harmed and He is with you always. Now, of course, moms and dads and bike helmets are important too. God has blessed us with people and things that keep us safe, and we are to listen to our parents and use the things in our life designed to protect and heal us. Just remember that God is the real protection behind the safety pad.

22 Bible Block and Tackle

God is our strength.

Active Ingredient

1 Chronicles 29:12, Romans 5:3–5

Hypothesis

Have you ever worked and worked to get the lid off a pickle jar only to hand it to someone who hardly touches it and off the lid comes? There are several tools that make your grip on jar lids stronger. This experiment demonstrates a simple machine. It can't remove a pickle jar lid but it can increase your strength.

Lab Equipment

- Two brooms
- A jump rope
- Two volunteers

Procedure

Hold the brooms, one in each hand, with the tops touching the floor. Ask the volunteers each to grab hold of a broom and try to pull them apart. This should be relatively easy for them. Now tie one end of the jump rope around the bottom of one broom. Wind the rope around the two broomsticks. Weave the ropes in and around the broomsticks.

Ask the volunteers to pull the broomsticks apart, but this time you pull on the rope. You should have little trouble keeping the broomsticks together.

Results

When you pull the rope, you exert a small amount of force over the long distance of the rope, and this makes your effort more effective. Your force is more effective than that of your friends because their force is exerted over a shorter distance.

With the broomsticks and the rope, you have created a block and tackle or a double pulley. This is a simple machine that can be used to do big jobs such as lifting and lowering heavy loads.

Application

The rope weaved in, out, and around the broomsticks was a simple way to enhance your strength. The Bible verse tells us that in God's hands are strength and power to give strength to all. He does not hesitate to give us strength.

While the block and tackle will enhance your physical strength, there is another kind of strength you need in your life. You could call it strength of character. People with strong character make good decisions and survive difficult times more easily than others.

Sometimes children have difficult things happen in their lives. As children of God you are not protected from illness, death, or divorce. These things can and do happen to God's children. Bad things happen because the world is full of sin. The children of God have the strength of God to help them.

Notice in the Bible verse from Romans that suffering produces perseverance and character. But suffering doesn't stop with character; suffering eventually leads to hope. Suffering itself does not make us strong, God makes us strong. The more you suffer the more you realize that you can have hope in the strength of God. You have assurance that God will be with you through difficult times in your life. With God woven in and around your life, you are strong.

23 It Only Takes a Spark

The love of God is for sharing.

Active Ingredient

Philemon 7, 2 Corinthians 4:16

Hypothesis

Some people have a laugh that is contagious. You hear them giggle and you can't help joining in even if you are not sure what is so funny. People who are happy and friendly and loving are easy to be around, and their attitude spreads.

Static electricity can be passed around too. Give these experiments a try and make some sparks.

Lab Equipment

- A cool, dry day
- A head of clean hair
- A piece of paper
- A Ping-Pong ball
- A small piece of wool or synthetic fabric

Procedure

Tear up the paper into fingertip-sized pieces. Run the comb through your hair several times and quickly hold it near the bits of paper. The paper should jump up to stick to the comb.

Recharge your comb by rubbing it with the fabric. Make the Ping-Pong ball move by placing the comb close to it and slowly moving the comb forward.

Results

Static electricity is responsible for the movement of the paper and the Ping-Pong ball. When you run the comb through your hair or with the fabric, electrons move from one to the other, leaving an electrical charge. Charged objects attract other objects that are neutral or oppositely charged. Objects that have the same charge will repel, which is why you can make your hair stand on end when you comb your hair on a dry day.

Application

Just like the paper and the Ping-Pong balls were attracted to the comb, you are attracted to the love of God. God's love is a special love that only He can give. It is a love that sent His Son to die in your place. God's love makes you feel especially good because it is unconditional. God loves you no matter what you do, no matter what happens to you.

God is always there for you. When you are happy, He celebrates with you. When you are sad, He comforts you. When you are worried, He calms your fears. God's love is a perfect love. It is a love that recharges you every day.

The love of God in your life helps you show love for the people around you. Christians can't love each other like God loves us, only He can do that. However, you can show Christian love and care for others. You can celebrate with, comfort, calm, and renew the people in your life with the love you have for each other. You can do this because of the love God has for you.

When you are sad or worried, being alone makes it harder to live through these feelings. When someone prays with you or hugs you or sends you a card, it doesn't make the sad feelings go away, but it does make them easier to handle. God's love is a love that is for sharing. Because He cares for you, you are able to recharge others with your love and care for them. Then they can spread God's love to someone else who needs it.

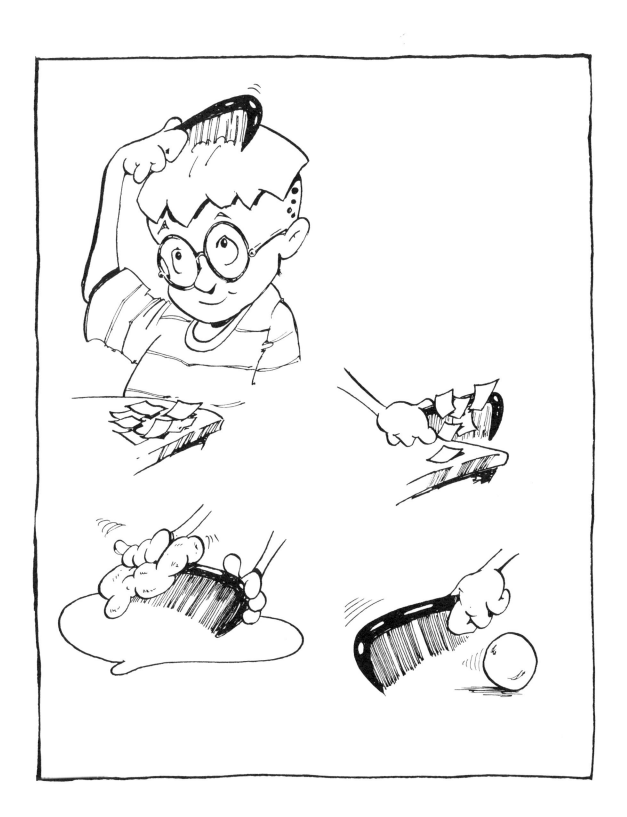

24 The Invisible Shield

Sanctification is a gift.

Active Ingredient

1 Corinthians 6:11, John 17:17–19

Hypothesis

What would your friends say if you told them that you could plunge a crumpled paper towel into a tub of water and it would not get wet? Your friends would want to know how you were going to protect that paper towel from the water. This experiment shows one way to accomplish this feat.

Lab Equipment

- Tub of water
- Clear glass
- Paper towel

Procedure

Crumple the paper towel and stuff it in the glass. It needs to be secure enough that it will not fall out when the glass is turned upside down. Hold the glass by the bottom and sink it upside down into the tub of water. Hold the glass in the water for a short time and carefully lift the glass. You need to keep the glass straight throughout this experiment. Pull the paper towel out of the glass and examine.

Results

Stuffed into the bottom of the glass with the paper towel is a layer of air. The air is lighter than water and cannot escape when the glass is submerged in the tub. Water cannot enter the glass to soak the paper towel because of the layer of air.

Application

One of the ways God protects you is called sanctification. To be sanctified means you have been set aside and made holy. You are sanctified when you are baptized and the Holy Spirit works in your heart. God sets you apart as His child. He calls you by name and you are His.

The paper towel is protected from the water by a layer of air. Because the water is heavier than the air, it cannot get past the air to soak the paper. You are protected by God's grace. His grace surrounds you and separates you from the world. You have been set aside as a child of God.

Being "set aside" makes you different from people who do not know God. You may look the same and like the same things but your faith makes you distinct. God's love for you and your faith in Him are the most important things in your life. This has an effect on everything you say or do. You are different because you have been chosen by God.

You can never be holy on your own. Because of the saving love of Jesus and the work of the Holy Spirit, you are sanctified and made holy in God's eyes. Nothing can penetrate that protective layer.

25 Seeing Straight

See the world with faith-dimensional eyes.

Active Ingredient

John 20:29, 1 Corinthians 13:12

Hypothesis

Have you ever wondered why God gave you two eyes? It's obvious you need two ears so you can hear in two directions, but your eyes are on the same side of your head. Maybe you should have one in the front and one in the back so you can see both ways?

This experiment will go a long way to explain how you use two eyes to see better than with one alone.

Lab Equipment

- A piece of poster board with a ½" hole cut in the center
- A pencil
- A volunteer

Procedure

With the pencil in one hand and the poster board in another, and with your hands as far apart as possible, put the pencil into the hole. With both eyes open this should be easy. Now close one eye and try to put the pencil in the hole as quickly as before.

Results

With two eyes you have stereoscopic vision. Each eye has a slightly different view, which allows your brain to judge distance by comparing the two views. With two eyes open you can see in three dimensions. With only one eye open, your view is more like a two-dimensional photograph, and distance is harder to judge.

Application

There are many things that happen in this world that you do not understand. Why are innocent people killed? Why do people get sick? Why do people you love die? You know that bad things in our world happen because of sin and its consequences, but that doesn't help you understand when something happens to someone you love.

What you see in the world you see only with your eyes. You cannot see things the way God sees them. Only God knows how everything fits together in His plan. Sometimes He lets you know why certain things happen, but often you have no explanation.

When you die and go to be with God in heaven, you will not be looking at God's plan with two-dimensional eyes. As the Bible verse says, "We will know fully." You will be with God and you will see Him "face to face." You will see and understand things with a new dimension. When you are with God, everything will make sense.

For now you see the world with *faith*-dimensional eyes. You do not understand why things happen, but you have been blessed with the gift of faith through your Baptism. This faith shows you that you do not have to see things the way God does to trust that He has a plan for you.

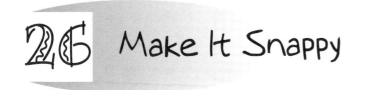

26 Make It Snappy

Be "hot" for the Lord.

Active Ingredient

Revelation 3:15, 2 Chronicles 25:2

Hypothesis

Have you ever done a job but not had your heart in it? Maybe Dad reminded you to take out the garbage and you chose to ignore him, hoping he would forget. When the second reminder came, you reluctantly got out of your chair and grumbled all the way into the kitchen, making sure your family understood the total lack of fairness in the whole situation. You were not exactly "hot" to take out the garbage.

Check out this experiment. You will find it is easy to get a rubber band hot.

Lab Equipment

- A large rubber band
- A volunteer lip

Procedure

Ask your volunteer to place the rubber band on his top lip. Ask him to make note of the temperature of the rubber band. Now ask the volunteer to grab the rubber band with both thumbs and forefingers with the thumbnails touching. Next, have your volunteer quickly stretch the rubber band several times. Then, ask him to place the rubber band on his lip again quickly to test the temperature of the rubber band. It should be warmer.

Results

If you use the model of molecules to explain rubber bands, then they stretch because the bonds between the molecules stretch. This movement of the bonds changes kinetic (movement) energy into thermal (heat) energy.

Application

In the Bible verse, Jesus warns a church that they should not be lukewarm. The church in Laodicea had become complacent, which means they were happy doing the bare minimum.

When you lose enthusiasm for a job, you can learn to be content with doing the bare minimum. You do what you have to but no more than that, and you make it clear you would rather be doing something else. House chores, homework, even jobs you do for pay can be done halfheartedly.

The second Bible verse refers to a king named Amaziah. He did what God asked but he did only the minimum. God's work still prevailed because God didn't need Amaziah to be wholehearted. But the kingdom did not realize the full measure of God's blessings. Later in his reign, Amaziah's halfheartedness showed up again when he brought some foreign gods home from battle. Amaziah did not have a strong commitment to the Lord and it showed in the way He did God's work.

Examine your faith life. Are you wholehearted or halfhearted? Do you eagerly dress and ready yourself for church and Sunday school or do you look for an excuse to sleep in? Do you set aside time to read and memorize God's Word or do you complain that suppertime devotions will make you late for your game? God is the one who can make your halfhearted faith life wholehearted. A wholehearted faith life is a blessing from God.

The rubber band became hot when it was stretched and used. When God stretches and uses your faith, you become "hot" for the Lord.

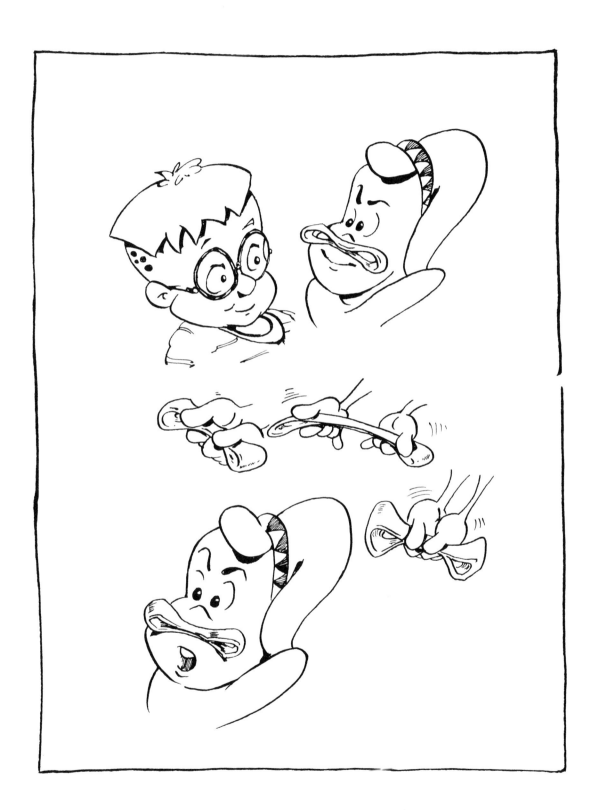

27 Don't Bury Your Bones

Use the gifts God gave you.

Active Ingredient

Romans 12:6, Philippians 2:13

Hypothesis

Have you ever received a gift that was so special that you wanted to hide it away to keep it safe? You absolutely did not want to have to share it, instead you wanted to keep it for yourself.

This experiment shows what happens when a sponge is buried. These "bones" were not kept safe buried in the sand.

Lab Equipment

- A small bucket of sand
- A small bucket of warm water
- Table salt or Epsom salt
- Kitchen sponges

Procedure

Cut the sponges into bone shapes. Bury the sponges about halfway down in a bucket ¾ full of sand. The second bucket should be about ½ full of warm water. Add salt and stir until no more salt can be added. Slowly pour the salt water into the bucket of sand. Let the bucket of sand and water sit in a warm dry place until the sand completely dries. This may take several hours or overnight. If the weather is humid, it may take a few days of drying time. When the sand is dry, dig out the bones.

Results

The salt particles from the salt water filled in the spaces in the sponges. The water evaporated, leaving behind the salt in the sponges.

With salt in the spaces the sponges became hard like bone.

In some real fossils, dissolved minerals have seeped into the spaces in animal bones or plant material. They dry and harden and the bones or plants become fossils.

Application

Jesus told a parable about servants who received talents (money) from their master. Two servants used the talents to earn more money, but one servant buried his because he thought he would keep it safe.

God blesses you with gifts. He blesses you with the gift of grace and He blesses you with talents or skills that you can use to serve Him. Some of God's children are good preachers or teachers or encouragers. You may or may not have these skills, but God has blessed you with talents that you can use to help others and to serve Him.

When you discover your gift, be careful not to bury it in the ground. Thank God for your talent and work to learn more about how to use it. God will show you ways that you can use your skills to do His ministry.

Think about what you are good at doing. Are you a good student, teacher, encourager, artist, writer, musician? How can you use these gifts from God to do His work here on earth? God not only blesses you with skills and talents, but He also gives you people in your life who can help you develop these talents. Then God goes one step further and helps you serve Him. Don't bury your talents like a bone. Use them to thank God for His many blessings.

28 The Levitating Marble

Lift up your friends in love.

Active Ingredient

John 15:12, Ecclesiastes 4:9–10

Hypothesis

There is nothing quite like a friend to cheer you up when you are feeling blue. Friends don't always fix things, but they can make you laugh and feel—for a little while anyway—that your world isn't as dark as you first thought. Caring words from a friend can lift you up.

Try this experiment to see how a marble can be lifted up by a jar full of sand.

Lab Equipment

- A small glass jar with a lid
- Sand
- Marble
- A volunteer

Procedure

Fill the jar about ¾ full of sand. Drop the marble into the jar and secure the lid. Ask the volunteer to try to move the marble from one end of the jar to the other. She might try shaking or rolling the jar. Now set the jar upside down on a table. Lightly tap the jar on the table and watch the marble slowly rise to the top.

Results

Gravity pulls the contents of the jar down. When you tap the jar, the sand is loosened and flows around the marble, lifting the marble up.

Application

The marble is heavier than the sand. You would not expect that the marble would "float" to the top. When you have a big problem in your life that weighs you down, it can be hard to believe that the words or actions of a friend can help to lift that weight. God is always there to help when we are sad or worried, but He has also blessed us with friends who can help us through difficult times.

You go to church to worship God. He deserves your praise and adoration. Praising Him reminds you of how wonderful God is. You also go to church to hear God's Word. His Word feeds your faith and prepares you to do His work. There is another reason why you worship together with others and that is to be part of a fellowship of believers. God has blessed you with people in your life. He uses people to help, encourage, and teach one another.

Sometimes you are the marble at the bottom of the jar. You may be sick or worried or afraid or sad. Your fellow Christians surround you with love and prayer and lift you up to the care of God.

Sometimes you are part of the sand that lifts up a fellow Christian who needs to hear about the love of God. With the help of God your words, prayers, or small deeds of kindness can encourage other people and help them through a difficult time.

29 Confuse Your Fingers

God won't let the devil fool you.

Active Ingredient

1 Corinthians 4:10, 1 Corinthians 2:14

Hypothesis

The best kind of prank is one that momentarily confuses a friend without hurting or embarrassing him. Practice this experiment and see if you can fool a friend's brain.

Lab Equipment

- A marble
- A volunteer

Procedure

Ask your volunteer to close her eyes. Have her cross her middle finger over the pointer finger on one hand and place that hand in the palm of the other. Tell her you will place something between her fingers and you want her to roll it around on her palm and tell you how many there are. Put a marble between her fingers. Until she opens her eyes and looks, she will insist that she feels two marbles.

Results

Your brain has a map of your skin and has coordinated this map with your sense of touch. When your sense of touch feels marbles on the outside of two fingers, your brain interprets that as being caused by two marbles because those sides of the fingers are not touching. It is interesting that the marble will still feel like two even after your eyes confirm that you are rolling only one marble.

Application

The devil would sure like to fool you. He shows you the world with all its glitter and tempts you to buy into it all. It is true that people who have won huge amounts in the lottery, or have fame and fortune through sports, or are known the world over as movie stars, look as if they have it all. But money and fame cannot make your life complete.

God makes your life complete through His gifts of forgiveness, faith, grace, and eternal life. The Holy Spirit turns you away from the temptations of the world and turns you toward the blessings of God.

The people of the world who do not know Jesus often do not understand why Christians do not crave the same things they do. They look at your life and the things that are important to you like kindness, trust, and a loving God, and they are confused. Because they lack the gift of faith, they cannot see what is really important in life. As a Christian you look like a fool to the world but you are a fool for Christ.

30 Polish Your Heart

Forgiveness changes your heart.

Active Ingredient

Acts 22:16, 1 John 1:9

Hypothesis

Have you ever made a mistake and tried to hide the evidence? The hardest stains to clean are the ones that will get you in deep trouble when Mom and Dad get home. This experiment will not help you get stains off the living room couch but it will make pennies shine.

Lab Equipment

- ¼ cup vinegar
- 1 tablespoon salt
- Two small bowls
- 1 cup soapy water
- Some dirty or dull pennies

Procedure

Pour the soapy water into one bowl. Try cleaning the pennies in the soapy water. No matter how hard you scrub, the pennies will not come clean. Now dry off the pennies and put them in a bowl with the vinegar and salt. Stir the salt to help it dissolve, and watch the pennies become clean and bright.

Results

Everyday dirt is not what makes the pennies brown. The pennies became dull when oxygen in the air combined with the copper on the pennies to form a copper oxide coating called tarnish. That is why the soapy water could not clean the brown off the pennies. The acid of the vinegar reacted with the salt to remove the tarnish from the copper.

Application

Just as food spilled on a couch will leave a stain, your sin stains your heart. You cannot hide your sin or wash it away. Even if you can hide your sin from other people, you can't hide it from God. The disciples did not know what Judas was up to, but Jesus did. Ananias and Sapphira sold their land and lied about their money to the apostles, but they couldn't hide it from the Holy Spirit.

You can't hide your sins and you can't clean them away either. Sometimes when you have disappointed a friend you can ease the bad feelings you have caused by doing something nice for that person. Most of us have tried bargaining with a sister or brother: "I'll give you my favorite car from my race car collection if you don't tell Mom what happened." Occasionally you can make things better or save yourself some grief, but the sin is still there, and you and Jesus know it.

Water could not clean the dirty pennies because the dull coating wasn't just dirt, it was a change in the chemistry of the penny. Sin isn't just dirt on your heart that can be dusted off or scrubbed away. Sin damages your relationship with God and other people. You can't wash it away with normal soap and water; you need a powerful change.

The blood of Jesus shed on the cross will react with the tarnish of your sin. Jesus' blood doesn't just wash you clean, it changes your heart too. Jesus forgives your sin, and the Holy Spirit, who comes to you through the wondrous waters of Baptism, works repentance in your heart. You become a shiny new penny with no trace of tarnish.

31 The Water Tightrope

Put your trust in God.

Active Ingredient

Proverbs 3:5, Psalm 33:22

Hypothesis

There is something about being nervous or afraid that makes you want to cling. You cling to a teddy bear in the dark, to a friend during a roller coaster ride, to the edge of your seat during a scary movie, and to your mother on the first visit to the dentist. Clinging to something or someone makes you feel a bit more secure.

Instead of fear, it is tension that causes water to cling to string in this experiment.

Lab Equipment

- A 12″ string
- A small nail
- A bowl
- A plastic or paper cup
- Water

Procedure

After making a small hole in the top of the cup, dampen the string and thread it through the hole. Tie a knot on the inside of the cup to secure the string. Fill the cup almost to the top with water.

With the cup in one hand, wrap the free end of the string around the index finger of your other hand. The hand not holding the cup should be over the bowl. Hold the cup high, stretching the string taut and slanting the string down toward the bowl. Slowly pour the water onto the string.

Results

You are watching surface tension in action. If you use the molecule model again, this experiment can be explained by the molecules at the surface of the water clinging together in a different way than the molecules within the liquid. The surface molecules form a tube that allows the rest of the water to flow down the string.

Application

There is something about clinging that makes you feel more secure. In fact, the American Sign Language sign for the word *trust* is both hands in fists with one on top of the other as if holding on to a rope stretching between you and God.

You do not have Jesus physically here to cling to, but the love and power of God are so strong that your needs are met. The Bible verse talks about the love of God resting upon you. You can imagine His love surrounding you like a blanket or the loving arms of a father.

When you are afraid, you can cling to God because He is all around you. He is with you wherever you go. He knows your every thought and need. You also have His Word to comfort and sustain you.

When the water clung to the string, it was led to its proper destination. When you cling to God and His Word, you are led to His will for you. He guides you in making decisions and in doing His work, and He goes one step further in blessing you with the courage to continue.

32 Peace like a River

God gives us peace.

Active Ingredient

John 16:33, 1 Peter 5:10

Hypothesis

Wheels make travel easier. This experiment demonstrates why rolling is smoother than sliding.

Lab Equipment

- Two cans
- Marbles

Procedure

Stack one can on top of the other. Try to turn the top or bottom can. Now place marbles on the top of the bottom can around the rim. Put the second can on top and try again to turn the can.

Results

At first the cans did not turn easily because of friction. Friction results from two surfaces sliding together. The marbles acted as ball bearings. Less friction is caused by rolling than by sliding because less surface area comes into contact, so the cans turned much easier.

Application

Some days your life feels like it is dragging. If you are sick, everything you do seems slower and requires more effort. When you are feeling good, you roll right through your day. Nothing can slow you down.

With the addition of the marbles the two cans turned with little effort. In both experiments the action of the cans was the same; the marbles alone made the difference.

You can understand that your attitude makes a big difference in how your day goes. A bad attitude causes friction with everyone around you. It doesn't work, though, to wake up each morning and simply declare you will have a good day. Faith in God gives you marbles that reduce the friction in your life. Those marbles are the gift of peace.

Peace is a calmness that settles in and smooths things out. Peace is knowing that God is in charge, that He knows what is happening and how it will all work out for you. Peace is knowing that He loves you dearly. This peace in your heart allows you to handle the bumps of life with a Christian attitude. You will not be happy with everything that happens to you, but God's gift of peace reminds you that He holds you in the palm of His hand.

ЗЗ Spread the Good News

Tell others about Jesus.

Active Ingredient

Acts 4:20, Acts 22:15

Hypothesis

The best kind of surprise is one that turns anger into delight-filled curiosity. Find an empty ketchup dispenser and do this trick. Air will help you spread some happiness.

Lab Equipment

- A plastic ketchup bottle like the ones on the lunch tables in school
- 2' of red embroidery floss
- A small bead

Procedure

Tie the small bead to the end of the embroidery floss and put it inside the ketchup bottle. Thread the other end of the string through the lid of the bottle from the inside out. Tie a knot at this end of the thread that is big enough to prevent the thread from sliding back into the ketchup bottle. Put the lid on the bottle and screw it tight. Squeeze the bottle and watch the thread squirt out of the bottle.

Results

The air in the bottle escapes when the bottle is squeezed. The air pulls the string out with it. The loose fibers on the thread act as sails to allow the air to push the thread. Air pressure, which is greater inside the bottle than out, also works to force the string out.

Application

When you squirt your fake ketchup at a friend, she will at first be upset. When she realizes there is no ketchup stain to deal with, her anger will turn to delight as she asks, "How did you do that?" Once you've got your friend's attention, you can explain how it works. By April Fools' Day, all your friends will have fake ketchup or mustard bottles to squirt. You have spread the news.

The Good News about the love of Jesus is a little like that. Some people don't want to hear about Jesus. They may think all you have to tell them is that they should go to church and follow a bunch of rules. If you squirt them with the Gospel, they might be grumpy about it.

But you know that the Good News about Jesus is more than church and commandments. The really Good News is the Gospel. The Gospel is what God has done for you. The Gospel is Jesus dying and rising so He can take away your sins and take you to heaven. The Gospel is God loving you no matter what you do. The Gospel turns grumpiness into happiness.

Just like the air shot the string out of the bottle, the Holy Spirit helps you spread the word about Jesus. When people hear God's Word and feel His forgiveness, they want to spread that good feeling too.

34 Find the True Color

God knows you better than you know yourself.

Active Ingredient

Matthew 10:30–31, Romans 8:26

Hypothesis

When you wear a mask, you keep your face hidden from other people. Even without masks it is hard for us to know what other people are really like. This experiment will reveal the colors we cannot see that make up the colors in markers.

Lab Equipment

- Coffee filters
- A water soluble black marker
- A cake pan
- Water

Procedure

Using the marker, color a black strip around the outside edge of the coffee filter. Use a water soluble marker, not a permanent marker. The cheaper the quality of the marker, the better the results. Fold the filter in half two or three times until you can form a cone. Fill the cake pan with ½" or so of water and stand the coffee filter cone in the water. Observe what happens to the color circles as the water moves up the filter.

Results

This procedure is called chromatography, which is a technique for separating chemicals through absorption into a liquid. Different chemicals have different absorption rates. When water was absorbed into the coffee filter, it separated the different inks used to make the marker.

Application

When you use a marker, you do not see all the colors used to make that specific color. When someone looks at you, he can't see all the thoughts that are inside you. You keep feelings, wishes, and dreams hidden from other people, but God knows you better than you know yourself. The Bible says that God knows how many hairs you have on your head, and He knows all your thoughts and feelings.

This can be a bit scary if you think about it. God knows all your nasty, mean thoughts as well as your fears and your hopes for what you want to be when you grow up. Remember that God loves you no matter what. He loves you and forgives you even when you think bad things. And He always gives you another chance to say you're sorry and to do better. He loves you and cares for you even when you are afraid. And He wants what is best for you when you have hopes for your life.

Jesus tells you that God knows you so well that the Holy Spirit even prays for you when you do not understand what to ask for or what you need. When you are sad, worried, hopeful, or angry God knows, understands, and can answer even a prayer you are not able to pray. God knows you better than you know yourself.

35 Hang on for the Ride

Trust in God always.

Active Ingredient

Psalm 23:4, Psalm 20:7

Hypothesis

Whom or what do you trust? Do you trust your high-powered name-brand shoes to help you make a basket? Do you trust your best friend to keep your deepest secret? Do you trust your coach to help your team win the championship? Do you trust your parents to always be there for you?

Try this experiment and see if you can figure out what keeps the coin from sailing across the room.

Lab Equipment

- A small coin
- A wire coat hanger
- A metal file

Procedure

Using the metal file, file a flat place on the bottom of the hanger for a coin to rest. Hang the coat hanger from your finger. Balance the coin carefully on the middle of the bottom wire of the coat hanger. Swing the hanger back and forth, gradually increasing the momentum until the hanger makes a complete circle with the coin remaining on the wire.

Note: This procedure requires a steady hand and some practice. Centrifugal force can also be demonstrated with a ball inside a small plastic bucket with a handle. Tie string to the handle and, with the ball inside, whirl the pail in circles.

Results

Centripetal force causes spinning bodies to move toward the center of the circle. Centrifugal force causes objects to move away from the center. Your motion keeps the hanger spinning, and centrifugal force causes the coin to press against it. While the hanger is spinning, this force equals the force of gravity and prevents the coin from dropping.

Application

The world tells us to put our trust in many things. Often this trust is misplaced. Expensive shoes, for instance, cannot make you a sports legend. Other times the trust is partially earned. Knee pads can go a long way to protect you, but they can't prevent every injury.

Putting your trust in your parents is a good thing. God gave you parents to love, protect, and teach you. Parents are sinners, though, just like you are, and sometimes they don't live up to their promises.

With God it is different. Your trust in Him is never misplaced, disappointed, or discouraged. He always comes through on His promises. There is more to your trust in God than the fact that God is completely dependable. The coin does not cling to the wire of the coat hanger of its own accord. The force generated by the spinning keeps it there. Likewise, you do not trust God on your own. God is not only steadfast and faithful, He also gives you the ability to trust Him. God is both trustworthy and trust-giving.

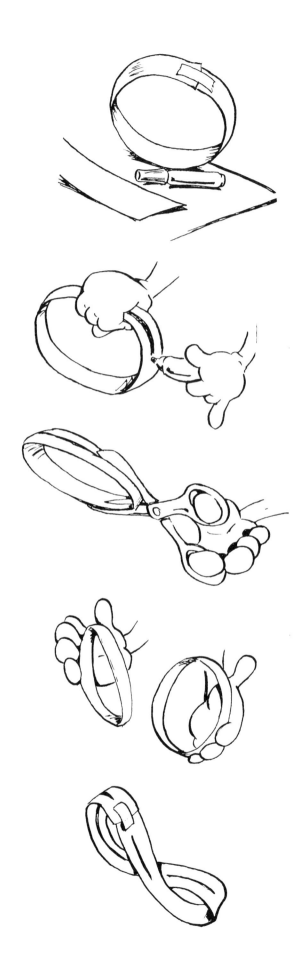

36 The Forever Circle

God never changes.

Active Ingredient

Hebrews 13:8, Matthew 28:20

Hypothesis

Can you cut a circle in half and have it still be a circle? Can you draw a line on one side but have the line show up everywhere? Explore the unique properties of a Moebius strip.

Lab Equipment

- Two strips of 1″ × 10″ paper
- Scissors
- A marker
- Tape

Procedure

Tape the ends of one paper strip together to form a circle. With a marker, draw a line down the middle of the strip all the way around the circle. With your scissors, cut the circle on this line. This should result in two circles.

Now try it again with the other paper strip. This time give one end a half turn before you tape it to the other end to form a circle. Starting at one end, draw a line down the middle of the strip all the way around the circle. Do you

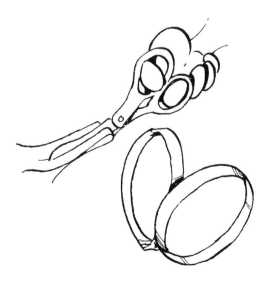

notice anything different? Cut on the line with your scissors. When you are finished cutting you should still have one circle.

Results

The second paper circle is a one-sided, one-edged Moebius strip, named after a mathematician who discovered it. The first circle had an inside and an outside, but twisting the paper before taping the second circle created a circle with only one side. You know it is one-sided because there is no need to turn the paper over to draw a marker line that is everywhere on the paper circle. When you cut the plain paper circle, you end up with two circles. When you cut the Moebius strip, you still have one circle.

This math is put to practical use with fan belts. Belts that have a half twist wear out more evenly and slowly because both sides of the belt are being used.

Application

When you cut the Moebius circle in half, you still had a circle. No matter what happens in your life, no matter how you change, God will always be the same. He created you, He loves you, He sent Jesus to save you. These things will always be true regardless of what happens in the world or in your life.

God will not change the rules on you. The words He wrote to you in the Bible are the same as the day they were recorded. Even if society changes its mind about what is acceptable and normal, God will not change. You can take comfort in that.

The Moebius strip has only one side. God is not two-sided like the plain circle. He is faithful to you and you can depend on that. When you sin, He loves you. When you serve Him, He loves you. When you are sick or hurting, He loves you. He is always the same. He is always with you.

37 Fingerprint Fun

You are unique.

Active Ingredient

Genesis 1:27, Psalm 139:13–14

Hypothesis

When you look at yourself in the mirror, do you look like anyone in your family? Do you look like anyone else you know? The Bible says you were created in God's image. Does the image you see in the mirror remind you of what you know about God? This experiment shows how you are different from anyone else in the world.

Lab Equipment

- Powder
- A fine paintbrush
- Clear tape
- Shiny black paper

Procedure

First make a fingerprint on an object. Use something smooth and easy to clean. Dust lightly with talcum powder. Gently blow away the excess powder. Brush the powdered spot very lightly with the brush to reveal the print. You must be very gentle to avoid damaging the print. This will take some practice. Place a piece of clear tape over the print to lift the remaining powder. Stick the tape on the shiny black paper.

Note: A faster way to get a print for viewing is to dust your thumb with powder and stick it to the tape. Then stick the tape to the black paper. This is does not stain like a stamp pad.

Results

Your skin has many tiny pores that allow oil to reach the surface and evaporate. You leave behind oil and perspiration on everything you touch. The powder sticks to the oil but not to the rest of the surface, revealing your special print.

Application

Take a close look at the fingerprint on the paper. Take a minute to study the lines. Compare the lines on your finger to those on the finger of a friend. If you study lots of fingerprints, you will see patterns that repeat but no two fingerprints are the same.

When you compare yourself to the other people in your life, you see some similarities. Your brother and you have the same kind of nose, which just happens to be like Grandpa Bob's nose. You and your best friend both love anchovy and mushroom pizza. Or you and your dad are both good musicians. When God made people, He made some things alike between people so you would have special connections to the loved ones in your life.

Even though you may be like people in your family, God also made you a unique person who is different from anyone else. Your fingerprint and that of another person may have similar swirls or loops but no one has a print exactly like yours. God knows you and loves you and He knows how you are different from anyone else.

There is something else that is special about the way God made you. He made you in His own image. This doesn't mean God has fingerprints like you do. God made you different from the other animals. You bear His imprint. You have a special relationship with Him.

Your sin ruined this relationship, but Jesus became man and took on fingerprints. You usually associate fingerprints with crime scenes. But you won't find Jesus' fingerprints on any sins. He lived a perfect life and restored your unique relationship with God. Because of Jesus, you are once again "in His image."

38 A House Built on Solid Ground

God blesses His children with gifts.

Active Ingredient

Romans 12:5, Ephesians 4:11–13

Hypothesis

Each part of a house—the walls, the ceilings, the doors, windows, and foundation—are together what makes a house strong and useful. In this experiment a toothpick and newspaper are weak when separate but strong together.

Lab Equipment

- Sheets of old newspaper
- Toothpicks
- Masking tape

Procedure

Spread one sheet of newspaper flat on the floor. With a toothpick across one corner, roll the newspaper very tightly around the toothpick until you reach the opposite corner. Secure with tape. Repeat this process until you have the desired number of paper dowels to build your structure.

Results

Neither the paper nor the toothpick are strong by themselves. Rolled together very tightly they become much stronger than when they are separate. Rolled together they form a cylinder, a very strong shape. The paper dowels, when taped together to form a structure, are also stronger together than apart.

Application

The newspaper dowels have formed a paper structure similar in some ways to a real building. The individual parts of a real building are not necessarily strong. A large steel beam can hold quite a bit of weight but not as much

as when it is combined with other beams to make a building or a bridge.

When you work alone against the world, you are not very strong. You are stronger when girded with the faith God gives you. In addition to faith, God has blessed you with special gifts to use to do His work. Other people in your church family have been blessed with gifts too. Not everyone can do the same things well. God blessed us each differently so His children can learn from and lean on one another.

When Christians work together and use their gifts to glorify God, they build up the body of Christ. Because of the blessings of God, the church is stronger when its members work together to do God's work.

The devil attacks the church with evils that act like floods, fires, or tornados on a building. God protects His church, strengthens His church, and supports His workers with the gifts of each member. Working together and working with God, the church can withstand anything the devil tries.

39 Like a Rushing Wind

The Holy Spirit works in us.

Active Ingredient

1 John 4:13, John 14:26

Hypothesis

We can't see air and unless it moves we don't feel it either. When air moves, it is called wind. This experiment lets you see air in action.

Lab Equipment

- A lamp
- A pencil
- A piece of paper
- Scissors
- A straight pin

Procedure

Cut the paper into a circle with a diameter of 3–3 ½", then cut the circle into a spiral strip about ½" wide. If the lamp shade is not open on the to,p take it off to expose the bulb. Turn on the light and wait a minute or two until the bulb is hot. When the lightbulb gives off heat, hold the pencil with the spiral over the bulb so the spiral can turn without bumping into the shade or your hand.

Results

The bulb heats the air around it. The warm air rises and causes a small wind, which turns the spiral.

Application

You can go for days without food and for hours without water, but going without air for even minutes will result in permanent injury or death. Your body needs a constant supply of air.

You need the Holy Spirit too. You can't see Him or feel Him but just like air you see the Holy Spirit working. God the Father created the world, God the Son came to earth to save you, and God the Holy Spirit came into your heart at your Baptism to give you faith.

We can't see air but we feel it filling our lungs when we breathe. The Holy Spirit fills our hearts with faith, then nurtures and sustains that faith.

When the air around us is warm, it warms our body also. The Holy Spirit warms us by making us strong and encouraging and comforting us as God's children.

We feel air when it moves as wind. We feel the Holy Spirit moving us to serve God and to tell others about the saving love of Jesus. Without air we cannot live, without the Holy Spirit we cannot live for Jesus.

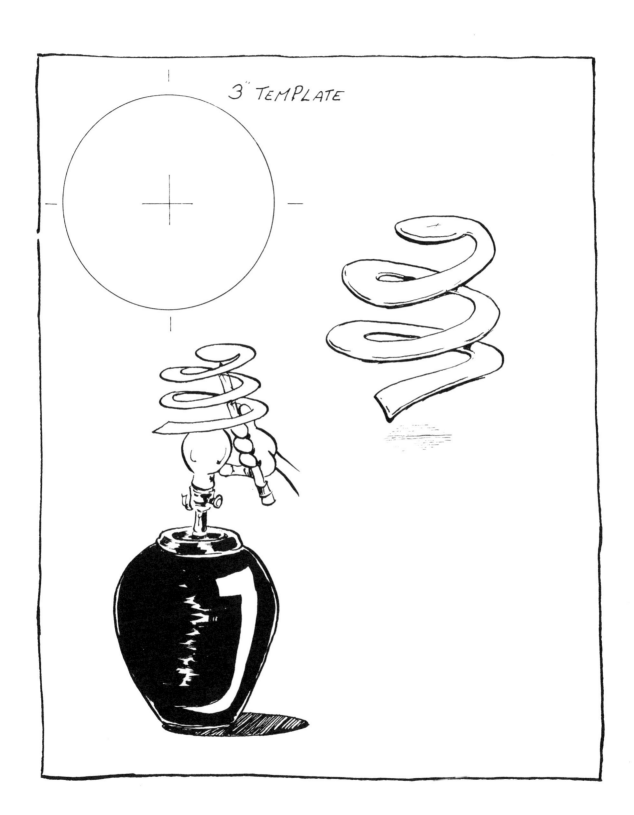

3" TEMPLATE

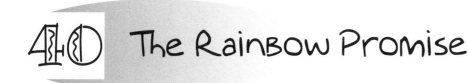

40 The Rainbow Promise

God keeps His promises.

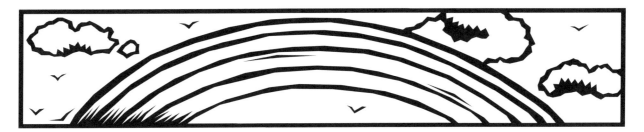

Active Ingredient

1 John 2:25, 2 Corinthians 1:20

Hypothesis

It can be hard to keep your promises. Some promises are easy and some are impossible to keep. In this experiment, a mirror, a flashlight, and some water will help you make a reminder of God's promise to us.

Lab Equipment

- A mirror
- A baking pan
- Water
- A flashlight

Procedure

Fill the pan half full of water. Set the mirror in the water so it is partially submerged. Shine the flashlight into the water onto the mirror. Move the flashlight and the mirror, experimenting with the angles until you are able to shine a rainbow on the wall or on a screen.

Results

When the light shines through the water onto the mirror, the reflection bends. White light contains all colors but different colors bend to form different angles so a rainbow is formed.

Application

Remember the rainbow from the story of Noah and the ark? God put the rainbow in the sky as a sign of His promise to never completely flood the earth again. Now when you see rainbows in the sky, you are reminded of God's many promises to you.

The Bible is full of God's promises: promises He has made, promises He has fulfilled, and promises He continues to keep. When you see a rainbow, let each color remind you of a different promise of God. He promises to always love you, to protect you, to give you strength and courage. And He promises to forgive you and bless you with spiritual gifts. God's promises are many and beautiful and faithful.

All the colors of the rainbow combine to remind us of God's greatest promise. He promised Adam and Eve that He would send a Savior. He kept that promise, and because of what Jesus did for us, we have the promise of eternal life in heaven with Him. The rainbow in the heavens reminds us of God's promise of salvation.

Index